MARX

BULLET GUIDE

Hodder Education, 338 Euston Road, London NW1 3BH

Hodder Education is an Hachette UK company

First published in UK 2012 by Hodder Education

This edition published 2012

Database right Hodder Education (makers)

Artworks (internal and cover): Peter Lubach
Cover concept design: Two Associates

Also available in ebook

British Library Cataloguing in Publication Data: a catalogue record for this title is available from the British Library.

10 9 8 7 6 5 4 3 2 1

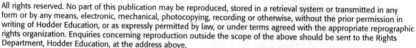

The publisher has used its best endeavours to ensure that any website addresses referred to in this book are correct and active at the time of going to press. However, the publisher and the author have no responsibility for the websites and can make no guarantee that a site will remain live or that the content will remain relevant, decent or appropriate.

The publisher has made every effort to mark as such all words which it believes to be trademarks. The publisher should also like to make it clear that the presence of a word in the book, whether marked or unmarked, in no way affects its legal status as a trademark.

Every reasonable effort has been made by the publisher to trace the copyright holders of material in this book. Any errors or omissions should be notified in writing to the publisher, who will endeavour to rectify the situation for any reprints and future editions.

Hachette UK's policy is to use papers that are natural, renewable and recyclable products and made from wood grown in sustainable forests. The logging and manufacturing processes are expected to conform to the environmental regulations of the country of origin.

www.hoddereducation.co.uk

Typeset by Stephen Rowling/Springworks

Printed in Spain

MARX

BULLET GUIDE

Robert Anderson

For my nephew Henry, a revolutionary in his own way!

About the author

Robert Anderson is a freelance teacher, writer, editor and translator. He studied modern languages at the University of Exeter and went on to live in France for a number of years.

He has taught in schools in France and the UK and has worked in educational publishing for more than a decade. He has written a wide variety of children's and adult's books, including a series of books on design icons for London's Design Museum, as well as online courses for the Tate Gallery.

Contents

Introduction

Karl Marx (1818–83) was undoubtedly one of the **most influential thinkers** of the modern age. His ideas – both his **critique of capitalism** and his **utopian vision of the communist society** – helped unleash a century's worth of revolution, ideological conflict, and social and political experiment. Under the impact of communism – or at least interpretations of it – millions of people's lives would be transformed, sometimes for the better and sometimes, undeniably, for the worse.

As a result, Marx is perhaps also one of the **most reviled thinkers** of modern times. In the West, especially during the Cold War, he became a bugbear – the **ultimate enemy** of freedom and liberalism. The pompous statues of him set up in many Eastern bloc cities hardly helped his case – in them, he looked startlingly like some Old Testament patriarch, dispensing rules and regulations to the masses.

For this reason, it is important not to confuse Marx's ideas with the use that was subsequently made of them nor the man with the clichés that have subsequently grown up around him. In this short book, we will focus our attention most insistently on Marx himself and the ideas that he developed in brilliant, insightful, painstaking works such as *Capital*. Marx, we will discover, was above all a humanist, passionately devoted to challenging conservative thinking and **liberating human potential**.

1 The age of revolutions

Challenging times

In Europe, the late eighteenth and early nineteenth centuries was an era of **unprecedented rapid social change**. New industrial processes and machines led to the proliferation of factories that required a **mass urban workforce**. City populations boomed as birth rates rose and people migrated from the countryside in search of work.

In the wake of the **French Revolution** of 1789 and the decline of autocratic regimes came new ideas about how society should be organized and regenerated. Urban overcrowding and poverty – a by-product of the **factory system** – too, helped fire political unrest across Europe, and mass working-class movements such as Chartism were born.

In Europe, the late eighteenth and early nineteenth centuries was an era of unprecedented rapid social change

Some statistics

The population of Manchester – the world's leading industrial city at that time – grew from c. 25,000 in 1772 to c. 455,000 in 1851. Only four out of every ten children in the city reached the age of five, owing largely to disease, malnutrition and poor medical care.

We will begin this chapter with a timeline, setting Marx's life in its historical context. We will also look at:

* the development of the factory system
* the Chartist movement in Britain
* 1848 – the 'Year of Revolutions'.

Marx in context

1775   The Scot James Watt's improved steam engine is patented: a key invention of the **Industrial Revolution**, it enables the rapid development of the **factory system**, initially in Britain and later across Europe and North America.

1789   The **French Revolution** overthrows the monarchy and adopts the Declaration of the Rights of Man and the Citizen; alongside the call for the right to **liberty** was the right to **property**.

1815   Napoleon, the Emperor of France, is defeated at Waterloo by the combined forces of Britain and Prussia, bringing to an end more than **two decades of intermittent European wars**.

1818   Marx is born in Trier, Prussia (now Germany).

1838   The beginning of **Chartism** in Britain – Europe's first mass working-class political movement.

1848	Marx and Engels publish *The Communist Manifesto*. In this **'Year of Revolutions'** mass uprisings take place across Europe. In a few countries, liberal reforms are instituted, but in most (e.g. France) there is a powerful conservative backlash.
1861	A united kingdom of Italy is declared.
1864	The **International Workingmen's Association ('the First International')** is formed, uniting working-class socialist, communist and anarchist groups across Europe.
1867	Marx publishes *Capital*.
1869	**The Social Democratic Workers' Party** is formed and is active across Germany.
1870–71	Prussia defeats France in the **Franco-Prussian War** and a new unified German state – the German Empire – is proclaimed; the **Paris Commune** briefly institutes working-class rule.
1881	The **Social Democratic Federation** is founded in Britain, directly inspired by Marx.
1883	Marx dies in London.

5

The factory system

The Industrial Revolution, which started in Britain in the late eighteenth century, was characterized not only by revolutionary **new technologies** such as Richard Arkwright's water frame for spinning cotton (patented in 1768) and James Watt's steam engine (1775) but also by its **transformation of working practices and conditions**.

The **'factory system'**, as it is known, had the following characteristics:

* Because of the bulky new machinery, workers were gathered together in one centralized building in a town or city – the **factory**; previously, cotton spinners, for example, had worked at home or in small workshops.
* **The division of labour** – the use of machinery broke production down into different, repetitive tasks that often required limited skill.

6

- **Long hours** – Workers typically worked 6 days a week and from dawn until dusk.
- **Few rights** – As factory workers were deskilled, they could be easily hired and fired, and were poorly paid.

For workers, the factory system thus meant:

- a loss of independence and control
- a loss of pride in their work as a craft
- a loss of self-esteem – they were little more than pawns of the factory owners
- living in the poverty and squalor of overcrowded city slums.

The **psychological**, let alone the material, trauma inflicted by the factory system on workers was devastating.

● The factory system revolutionized the world of work, condemning factory workers to a life of stressful, dehumanizing wage labour

Chartism

The industrial working class – especially the skilled sectors of it – did not bear the iniquities of the factory system passively; very quickly they formed co-operatives and friendly societies to alleviate the worst effects of wage labour, while working men's organizations sought to educate and politicize their members. Out of these early glimmerings of **class consciousness** grew the **first working-class mass movement**, Chartism, the primary goal of which was universal male suffrage.

> **The whole struggle of the workers against the factory owners [...] has developed into the most conscious class struggle which the world has ever seen ...**
>
> Marx on Chartism

Launched in 1838, Chartism used or planned to use a variety of methods to further its aims during its 20-year history:

* **mass demonstrations and petitioning**
* **political organization** – sponsoring of radical (socialist) candidates for Parliament
* **concerted strike action**
* **revolution** – plans were made for the Chartist Convention to become a rival to Parliament and even for national uprising; the Newport Rising in 1839 may have been meant as the trigger for a wider armed rebellion.

While Chartism ultimately failed, it marks a decisive moment in the **development of a working-class politics**.

Engels and Chartism

Marx's close colleague, Friedrich Engels, became involved with Chartism in Manchester. This fired him to write his 'exposé' of the appalling working and living conditions in the city, *The Condition of the Working Classes in England* (1845).

The Year of Revolutions

In 1848 there was a wave of uprisings across Europe, as middle-class liberals and working-class radicals combined to oust reactionary regimes. For Marx and other left-wing activists and thinkers, the political ferment seemed to be the beginning of an **international revolution** that would bring in a new golden age.

January The first of the year's people's uprisings takes place in Sicily.

February In France, the middle-class liberal opposition, with the support of working-class socialists, overthrow the constitutional monarchy of Louis-Philippe.

March Leftist revolutions break out in the southern and western German states, with mass demonstrations and the institution of popular assemblies. Uprisings also break out in the Habsburg Empire (Austria–Hungary), mainly among subject peoples such as the Czechs and Slovaks.

June The working-class June Days Uprising in Paris.

In most countries conservative backlashes swiftly crushed working-class dissent and the radical programmes of the revolutionaries remained unrealized.

● 1848 – flying the flag of liberty!

Class conflict

With hindsight, Marx viewed the 1848 French Revolution as a classic example of class conflict. Soon after the February Revolution, the middle-class leaders of the new republic reined back on the radical proposals of their working-class comrades. On 23 June, thousands of working-class Parisians rose up against the government, but were brutally suppressed by the National Guard.

2 The young Marx

A life in exile

Karl Marx was far from being an 'ivory tower' intellectual. From his twenties he became actively engaged in **radical politics** and as a consequence spent most of his adult life in political exile from his native Prussia. He led a precarious career as a **writer** and **journalist**, and he and his family for ever teetered on the edge of poverty.

His life can be divided into two halves, their boundary marked by the failed revolutions of 1848 and Marx's self-imposed exile to London.

Karl Marx was far from being an 'ivory tower' intellectual

In this chapter we will look at:

* Marx's upbringing and student years
* Marx's work as a radical journalist
* the collaboration of Marx and Engels
* the crisis years of 1848–49.

● Marx has a reputation as an austere, wise patriarch, but in his youth in particular he was given to wild living, heavy drinking and womanizing

Upbringing and student years

1818 Karl Marx is born on 5 May in the German city of **Trier**, a city close to Luxembourg in the far west of present-day Germany and at that time part of the German state of **Prussia**. Marx is born into a prosperous family of Jewish descent; his father is a lawyer.

1835 He studies law, first at the University of Bonn and then, the following year, at the University of Berlin where he comes into contact with the philosophy of **Hegel** and his followers. He switches his studies from law to philosophy.

1836 He becomes secretly engaged to his childhood sweetheart, the aristocratic **Jenny von Westphalen** (1814–81).

1841 His involvement with the radical **Young Hegelians** hampers his academic career, but he is awarded a doctorate by the University of Jena.

The Young Hegelians

During the 1830s a group of young thinkers took up and developed the ideas of the philosopher Hegel (see Chapter 4). The Young Hegelians, as they were known:

* challenged the oppressiveness of the Prussian state, especially its use of religion as a tool of power, but hoped for a gradual, peaceful progresion towards constitutional monarchy
* founded a journal, the *Hallischer Jahrbücher*, to disseminate their ideas
* after 1840 became increasingly radical, variously adopting republican, atheist and communist standpoints.

During his time in Berlin, Marx became closely associated with the group, although he became impatient with their theorizing and argued for more **direct political action** and commitment.

The radical journalist

1842 Marx moves to Cologne (a city not far from Trier) and starts work on the radical *Rheinische Zeitung* (the *Rhinelander Newspaper*), first as a journalist and soon after as its editor.

1843 His controversial articles for the paper lead the Prussian authorities to ban the *Rheinische Zeitung*.

Later that year he finally marries Jenny von Westphalen and the couple move to Paris, which was home to many political refugees. Marx becomes ever more deeply involved in radical politics and continues to work as a radical journalist.

● Marx used his journalism both to address the injustices he saw and to make his living

18

1844 He begins his friendship with fellow German journalist and radical **Friedrich Engels** and they become involved with a secret revolutionary group of émigré German workers known as the Bund der Gerechten (**League of the Just**).

1845 Marx is expelled from France and goes to live in Belgium; Engels follows soon after.

1847 Marx and Engels transform the League of the Just into the **Communist League**, an international organization openly committed to revolution. The League holds two congresses in London, and at the second of these Marx and Engels are commissioned to write its **manifesto** (see Chapter 5).

Working men of all countries, unite!

Slogan of the Communist League

Marx and Engels

The collaboration of Marx and Engels is one of the great friendships and working partnerships of political history.

20

Engels' timeline

1820	Born into a wealthy family in Barmen, Prussia.
1842	Goes to work in one of his father's mills in Manchester, but becomes involved in Chartism.
1845	Publishes *The Condition of the Working Classes in England*.
1845–48	Works alongside Marx in the Communist League.
1849	Returns to Manchester, where he leads a double life as an industrialist and political subversive.
1870	Moves to London and, after Marx's death, becomes his literary executor.

Engels was undoubtedly the junior partner in their lifelong collaboration. He happily recognized Marx's genius and was prepared to help him in any way he could:

* Engels supported Marx **intellectually**, helping him to refine and clarify his ideas. He was one of the few people able to read Marx's handwriting and, after his friend's death, edited the second and third volumes of *Capital*.
* He supported him **financially**, using his allowance and income derived from his job at his father's mill in Manchester to support the straitened Marx family.
* He supported him **emotionally**, chiding Marx about looking after his health and keeping to his deadlines. The two friends sent each other hundreds of letters, packed with political speculation, gossip and schoolboy humour.

Through their 40-year friendship, Engels provided Marx with a **bedrock** on which his erratic genius could flourish.

1848–49: A turning point

The period 1848–49 marked a turning point in Marx's life. The popular unrest that broke out in many European countries through 1848 seemed to suggest that Marx's hopes for an international working-class revolution were about to be fulfilled.

1848

February *The Communist Manifesto* is published (see Chapter 5).

March After a brief imprisonment, Marx is exiled from Belgium as a political subversive; he goes to France where a new republic has replaced the monarchy.

April With other Communist League members, Marx returns to Germany in order to agitate for political change.

> **A spectre is haunting Europe – the spectre of communism.**
> *The Communist Manifesto*

June He starts publishing a daily newspaper, the *Neue Rheinische Zeitung – Organ der Demokratie* (the *New Rhenish Paper – Organ of Democracy*), which rapidly reaches a circulation of 5,000. Over the following months, as political unrest intensified across Prussia, the paper and Marx and his staff were frequently subjected to intimidation by the authorities.

1849

May The authorities finally shut down the *Neue Rheinische Zeitung*, prosecute many of the staff and deport Marx. Marx puts out a last defiant issue of the paper on 18 May, printed in red ink.

June Marx arrives in France, where, however, a counter-revolution is now in full swing.

August Marx is exiled to Brittany, but decides to move to England instead.

> **We have no compassion and we ask no compassion from you. When our turn comes, we shall not make excuses for the terror.**
>
> *Neue Rheinische Zeitung*, Issue 301, 18 May 1849

3 Marx in London

The radical thinker and family man

In the mid-nineteenth century London was the **biggest city in the world** and home to large communities of economic migrants from all over the British Isles and Europe. In 1851, some 26,000 of the capital's total population were from continental Europe.

The **inequalities** in living conditions between rich and poor were immense – with the vast majority living in insanitary, cholera-ridden slum dwellings where mortality rates were very high.

The inequalities in living conditions between rich and poor were immense

It was in this bustling, contradictory city that Marx spent the rest of his life, working haphazardly on his writing, lecturing and engaging in political activism, all while struggling to keep his family afloat.

In this chapter we will look at:

* Marx's work as a journalist and writer
* his family life and the careers of his children
* his involvement with the First International
* his final years and death.

In London we will get down to business.

Letter from Marx to Engels, encouraging him to join him in England

The German refugee

1850 The Marx family move to settled lodgings at **28 Dean Street, Soho**. Marx spends much of his time researching and writing in the British Museum.

1851 Marx begins to write for the liberal **New York Daily Tribune**, one of the USA's leading newspapers; he contributes articles for 10 years, although Engels often did a lot of the work.

1855 Marx's daughter, **Eleanor Marx** is born; his son, Edgar, dies of tuberculosis.

1856 Buoyed by inheritances from Jenny Marx's uncle and mother, the Marx family moves to a rather bigger, more comfortable house at **9 Grafton Terrace, Kentish Town**, then on the very edge of London.

Family life

Although Marx now earned a regular income from his journalism and received generous support from Engels, the Marx family lived precariously. Karl and Jenny Marx frequently had to resort to the pawnbrokers to tide them over, and often they could not afford to pay for medical care when their children fell sick. Three of the Marx children died during infancy and another, Marx's beloved son Edgar, died at the age of eight.

Despite such tragedies, the chaotic Marx household was largely a happy and affectionate one, even if dominated by Marx's sometimes overbearing and fiery personality.

Marx's wife and children

Marx's wife, **Jenny Marx** (née Baroness Joanna Bertha Julie von Westphalen), did not take part in his political activities, but remained loyal and supportive throughout their marriage, despite the many challenges and hardships she faced.

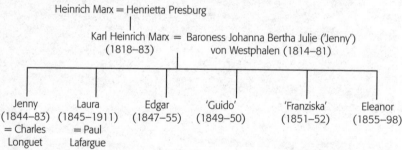

Heinrich Marx = Henrietta Presburg

Karl Heinrich Marx = Baroness Johanna Bertha Julie ('Jenny')
(1818–83)   von Westphalen (1814–81)

| Jenny (1844–83) = Charles Longuet | Laura (1845–1911) = Paul Lafargue | Edgar (1847–55) | 'Guido' (1849–50) | 'Franziska' (1851–52) | Eleanor (1855–98) |

The couple's surviving children grew up ardently committed to their father's ideas and led their own extraordinary lives:

Jenny Marx worked as a socialist journalist and married the former Communard Charles Longuet. She died of cancer in 1883. Her son, Jean, became a prominent socialist lawyer.

Laura Marx married the French socialist Paul Lafargue and with him became active in the French Workers' Party. In old age, in 1911, the couple committed suicide, because they felt they had nothing more to give to their party.

Eleanor Marx, alongside a brief career as an actress, was active in politics and, in 1884, alongside figures such as the designer William Morris, founded the Socialist League. In 1898 she committed suicide as the result of an unhappy love affair with another Socialist League luminary, Edward Aveling.

The political activist and writer

1864 Marx becomes involved in the **International Workingmen's Association** (IWA) and is elected to its general council at its first meeting at St Martin's Hall, London.

1866 The IWA holds its **first congress** in Geneva, Switzerland.

1867 Marx finally publishes the first volume of **Capital: Critique of Political Economy**, but continues to labour on its successive volumes until his death.

● Karl Marx spent much of his time researching and writing in the domed, book-lined Reading Room of the British Library in Bloomsbury

The International Workingmen's Association

Often known as the First International, the IWA was the **principal platform** for Marx's political activism in the second half of his life. Dedicated to the advancement of the working classes, the IWA brought together a wide range of political movements, encompassing trade unionism, communism, socialism and anarchism, and at its height in the 1870s may have had as many as **8 million** members internationally.

The IWA eventually became riven by conflict between two main groupings – the **communists** under the figurehead of Marx, and the **anarchists** under the Russian Mikhail Bakunin (1814–76). At the **Hague Congress** of 1872, the anarchists were finally ejected from the movement. The IWA subsequently moved its headquarters to New York and disbanded 4 years later.

Last years and death

Marx's final years were marked by **debilitating illness**, including bronchitis, and by grief caused by the death of family members. He became increasingly dependent on Engels and his youngest daughter, Eleanor, who worked as his secretary.

1872 The International Workingmen's Association moves its headquarters to New York City and later disbands.

1883 Jenny Marx dies of cancer. Marx dies on 14 March and is buried in **Highgate Cemetery** (East). Although well known and esteemed in radical circles, his funeral is attended by only 11 mourners.

The philosophers have only interpreted the world in various ways – the point however is to change it.

From the *Theses on Feuerbach* by Marx, part of the epitaph inscribed on his tomb

Principal works

1845 *The Holy Family* (with Engels) – a critique of the Young Hegelians

1848 *The Communist Manifesto* (see Chapter 5)

1867 *Capital*, Volume 1 – a study of the workings of capitalism (see Chapter 7)

1885 *Capital*, Volume 2 (edited by Engels)

1888 *The Theses on Feuerbach* (written 1845) – a critique of the ideas of Ludwig Feuerbach (see Chapter 4)

1894 *Capital*, Volume 3 (edited by Engels)

1932 *The German Ideology* (written with Engels in 1846) – includes Marx's most complete statement of his theory on history

4 Influences

New ideas, new directions

The intensity and rapidity of the societal changes in Europe during the late eighteenth and early nineteenth centuries helped stimulate a wealth of new ideas. **Economists** such as Adam Smith offered brilliant analyses of the capitalist system, while **social reformers** such as Robert Owen sought ways of tempering its effects on the lives of workers. In the turbulent wake of the French Revolution in 1789, too, came **radical movements** such as communism and anarchism that challenged the very basis of state and society.

The intensity and rapidity of the societal changes in Europe ... helped stimulate a wealth of new ideas

Above all, however, the young Marx was shaped by the **philosophy** of Georg Friedrich Hegel and his followers.

By developing and, to some extent, contesting these ideas, Marx was able to forge a **daring new synthesis** of economic, social and philosophical ideas that would change the world for ever.

In this chapter we will look at:

* the development of communism
* the key political and economic thinkers who influenced Marx
* the philosophy of Hegel and Feuerbach.

Communism before Marx

Communism is so closely associated with Marx that it is easy to believe that it only came into existence with him. In fact, **communistic** ideas and experiments can be traced back to ancient times, although the French Revolution provided them with a new impetus.

Key term: communism

The word 'communism' shares its etymology with the English word 'common' and so means 'shared' or 'held in common'. A core feature of communistic beliefs through the ages is the idea that resources and assets such as land should be owned and shared by the community, not by the private individual.

In *The Republic* (380 BCE) **Plato** describes an ideal city-state in which not only property but wives and children are held in common.

Radical Christian movements such as the Diggers in the sixteenth century and the Anabaptists in the seventeenth century believed that society should be based on shared ownership and that this ideal was implicit in the teachings of Jesus Christ.

During the French Revolution of 1789, while all the revolutionaries favoured a redistribution of wealth among the classes, some radicals, notably **Gracchus Babeuf**, militated for a society based on communal ownership, although they were ultimately routed.

> **The group of believers was one in mind and heart. No one said that any of his belongings was his own, but they all shared with one another everything they had.**
>
> The New Testament, Acts 4:32

Key political and economic thinkers I

Marx drew inspiration for his ideas from a wide range of political thinkers. While he did not always agree with their ideas, they provided the progressive intellectual climate in which his own could take root.

* In works such as *Le Contract social* (*The Social Contract*), the Enlightenment philosopher **Jean-Jacques Rousseau** (1712–88) often critiqued the institution of private property and praised the communal values of prehistoric hunter–gatherer societies.
* **Adam Smith** (1723–90) was a Scottish economist who, in *The Wealth of Nations* (1776), was among the first thinkers to analyse the economic and political changes brought about by the Industrial Revolution, especially the emergence of the new capitalist class.
* **Claude Henri de Rouvroy, compte de Saint-Simon** (1760–1825) was a French aristocrat who argued that the new industrial society necessitated a new political structure and looked forward to the social progress that he believed the new technologies would bring.

42

✳ **Robert Owen** was a Welsh-born manufacturer who sought to mitigate the effects of industrial society through the setting up of communal workers' villages, such as the model one he founded at New Lanark in Scotland (1800).

Key term: utopian socialism

In *The Communist Manifesto* Marx referred to reformers such as Robert Owen and Saint-Simon as **utopian socialists**, whose ideas grew from a generalized, idealistic desire to improve the condition of society and who often sought to implement their ideas in small-scale experiments such as Owen's New Lanark. As proposed by Marx and Engels, **scientific socialism**, by contrast, was rooted in a thoroughgoing analysis of capitalism as a historical struggle between the ruling class and the workers.

Key political and economic thinkers II

* **Louis Blanc** (1811–82) was a French socialist writer whose best-known work was the essay 'L'organisation du travail' ('The Organization of Work', 1839). He argued for the setting up of workers' co-operatives and famously stated the egalitarian mantra: 'to each according to their needs, from each according to their abilities'.

* **Charles Fourier** (1772–1837) argued that the factory system was dehumanizing and argued for the formation of small egalitarian communities called phalanstères.

* **Pierre-Joseph Prudhon** (1809–65) was a French anarchist who took part in the 1848 Revolution. His 1840 work *Qu'est-ce que c'est la propriété?* (*What Is Property?*) had a profound impact on the young Marx and is best known for its formulation 'property is theft'.

* The Russian anarchist **Michael Bakunin** argued for the dispersal of power throughout society and believed that a communist state would be just as tyrannical as a capitalist one. Often portrayed as Marx's arch nemesis, Bakunin provided Marx with a powerful counterpoint to his own ideas.

Key term: anarchism

Anarchism argues for a society 'without rulers' (the meaning of the Greek from which the term derives) in which people work freely for the common good without the need for a state and its institutions. Prudhon was the first to describe himself as an anarchist.

* It is important not to forget the crucial influence of **Friedrich Engels** on the ideas of his friend Karl Marx. Marx's reading of Engels' powerful work *The Condition of the Working Classes in England* (1845) – in which he exposed the human consequences of the Industrial Revolution – marked a key moment in the development of Marx's thought.

● Anarchists believe in a society in which no one has authority over others

Hegel and history

The Prussian philosopher Georg Wilhelm Friedrich Hegel (1780–1831) perhaps had the most profound impact on Marx, even if he was ultimately to contest many of his great forebear's fundamental ideas. The Russian revolutionary Lenin suggested that it was impossible to understand *Capital* without first understanding Hegel – a daunting task!

Hegel's influence is clearest in the two men's **view of history**. For Hegel, history was the evolution of a rational **'universal mind'** towards its most perfect expression across all forms of reality – whether the political state or in individual human consciousness. This evolution took place through an ongoing **dynamic interplay** between antagonistic forces and their eventual synthesis in a higher unity.

Marx took this profoundly optimistic vision of history – and its faith in human perfectibility – but brought it down to earth in his core ideas of **historical materialism** and the **dialectic** (see Chapter 6).

Feuerbach and materialism

Hegel's philosophy was **idealist** – that is, it was concerned with how abstract, metaphysical forces shape human history. Marx, by contrast, was a **materialist**, believing that historical development is caused by 'real-life' phenomena such as technology, the economy and culture. Marx was influenced by the work of the 'Young Hegelian' **Ludwig Feuerbach** (1804–72). An atheist, Feuerbach argued in *Das Wesen des Christentums* (*The Essence of Christianity*, 1841) that God does not shape humanity, but that humanity shapes God. Marx took up Feuerbach's ideas in his *Theses on Feuerbach* (1845, published posthumously), in which he criticized idealism and showed how the materialist standpoint squarely places responsibility for history and society **in human hands**.

5 The Communist Manifesto

A revolutionary document

In 1848 – the year of widespread revolutionary upheavals across Europe – a group of German political refugees in London published a **23-page pamphlet** entitled *Manifest der Kommunistischen Partei* (*Manifesto of the Communist Party*). It was soon redubbed *The Communist Manifesto*. This short work was to become one of the most influential political documents ever written. Its **searing analysis of capitalism** as a violent instrument of oppression and its **rallying cry for revolutionary change** had an impact, the power and import of which has not diminished to this day.

One of the most influential political documents ever written

In this chapter we will look at:

* the **early history** of the *Manifesto* and its opening salvo
* its **analysis of capitalism** as an instrument of oppression
* its call for **revolutionary change** (not reform)
* some **reactions** to the *Manifesto*.

Working men of all countries, unite!

A 'confession of faith'

The timeline of the *Manifesto*

July 1847   Engels is commissioned to write the *Communist Confession of Faith* – as a 'catechism' for the **Communist League** (the first draft of the *Manifesto*).

October 1847 Engels writes *The Principles of Communism* (the second draft).

1848   Marx reworks *The Principles* as *The Manifesto of the Communist Party*, which is published in London.

1850   **First English translation** of the *Manifesto* by the Scottish feminist Helen McFarlane.

1860(?)   First US edition.

1920   First Chinese edition.

The opening salvo

> **A spectre is haunting Europe – the spectre of communism. All the powers of old Europe have entered into a holy alliance to exorcise this spectre: Pope and Czar, Metternich and Guizot, French Radicals and German police-spies.**

With these opening words, the *Manifesto* announced the **arrival of communism** on the European stage.

The *Manifesto*, however, set out to show that communism:

* was *not* something to be **feared** (a 'spectre'), *but*
* a promise of **hope for the future** – for a fairer and more harmonious society.

Revolutionary road

Having launched their opening salvo, Marx and Engels went on to give an outline of their ideas – an **analysis of capitalism**:

> **Key term: class warfare**
> The notion of **'class warfare'** is one of the classic tenets of Marxism – for Marx it is an enduring phenomenon of pre-communist society. Feudalism, for example, is characterized by the struggle between lords and serfs.

* All of history could be shown to be a struggle between two classes – the **oppressors** and the **oppressed**.
* Under capitalism, the primary class struggle is between:
  » the bourgeoisie and
  » the proletariat …

and has become a brutal battle of life and death.

The proletariat will be the inevitable victor in the class struggle; capitalism will give way to **socialism** … and finally to **communism** in which all class strife, and indeed the class system, will 'wither away'.

> **Key term: the bourgeoisie**
> The middle-class owners of capital – of the means of production – who ruthlessly exploit the proletariat to accumulate wealth.

> **Key term: the proletariat**
> The workers who, despite being the **producers** of wealth, are kept in poverty and are disenfranchised.

The *Manifesto* ended with a rousing call to revolution:

Let the ruling classes tremble at a Communist revolution. The proletarians have nothing to lose but their chains. They have a world to win ... Workingmen of all countries, unite!

The ten steps towards socialism

The *Manifesto* is a strongly **utopian** (idealistic) document. While it provides an incisive analysis of contemporary conditions under capitalism, it is rather more vague when it comes to how the ideal society under communism is to be brought about.

Nonetheless, the *Manifesto* offers a list of **ten steps** that Marx and Engels believed necessary for the creation of the *socialist* state:

1 the abolition of landed property
2 the introduction of a progressive income tax
3 the abolition of inheritance
4 confiscation of the property of emigrants and rebels
5 the centralization of credit in a state bank
6 the centralization of transport
7 industry and agriculture to come under state control
8 all citizens to be liable to labour

9 the distinction between town and country to be dissolved and the
   population to be spread evenly throughout the land
10 the introduction of a free public education system.

We may feel that some
of these steps are quite
reasonable – the centralized
transport system, the
progressive income tax, and
the free public education, for
example. Others may strike
us as being draconian or even
hare-brained – the 'abolition'
of the difference between town
and country, for example.

● The abolition of town and country

Some reactions to the *Manifesto*

Initially the *Manifesto* received little attention and it was only later in the nineteenth century when Marx's ideas became better known that it became widely read. Since then it has become one of the most **contested** documents in human history, **admired** and **reviled** in roughly equal measure.

Here are two famous reactions to this revolutionary work:

This pamphlet, displaying greater genius than any other in world literature, astounds us even today by its freshness. Its most important sections appear to have been written yesterday. Assuredly, the young authors [Marx was 29, Engels 27] were able to look further into the future than anyone before them, and perhaps than anyone since them.

Leon Trotsky, Russian revolutionary

Most people who read *The Communist Manifesto* probably have no idea that it was written by a couple of young men who had never worked a day in their lives, and who nevertheless spoke boldly in the name of 'the workers'.

Thomas Sowell, US economist

What is your reaction to this document? Do you admire its idealism or are you horrified by its extremism? Or is your reaction mixed?

6 Economic theories

Historical materialism

In his economic theories Marx primarily sought to analyse and expose the **hidden mechanisms of capitalism**. To do so, he developed an **overarching perspective** on human history, which he saw as being driven by economic forces and relations.

Marx, however, is not a pure or 'scientific' economist. His major work on economics, *Das Kapital* (*Capital*: vol. 1 – 1867; vol. 2 – 1885; vol. 3 – 1894), is a vast compendium of ideas and theories drawing on his researches not only into economics but also into sociology, anthropology, politics, philosophy and literature.

In his economic theories Marx primarily sought to analyse and expose the hidden mechanisms of capitalism

Those who wish to explore Marx's economic ideas might like to try his shorter works that were based on lectures he gave to working men's associations: *Wage-labour and Capital* (1849) and *Value, Price and Profit* (1898, edited by Eleanor Marx). These essentially condense the ideas found in volume 1 of *Capital*.

In this chapter, we will look at:

* the materialist conception of history
* the forces and relations of production
* commodities and different kinds of value
* the 'mystery' of surplus value.

The materialist conception of history

As we saw in Chapter 4, Marx was influenced by Hegel's ideas about the **dialectic progression of history** – that is, its development towards the ideal through a repeated process of conflict and resolution. Hegel's notion was abstract and 'philosophical'; Marx, however, applied Hegel's idea to the **economic development** of human society.

According to Marx, so far there had been **four major phases** of economic development – primitive communism, ancient society, feudalism and capitalism. Each phase had its own pattern of growth, internal struggle and decline, eventually to be destroyed by its own inherent contradictions.

Crucially, the economic (or 'material') characteristics (the **substructure**) of each phase **underpinned** all the other characteristics of the phase – social relations, politics, art and so on (the **superstructure**).

Marx called his theory the 'materialist conception of history', which Engels neatly shortened to **'historical materialism'**.

Primitive communism
In this phase, hunter–gatherers work co-operatively and in harmony with nature to clothe and feed themselves. There are no classes and little or no private property

↓

Ancient society
In this phase, following the development of farming, society is divided between a wealthy warrior elite and a slave class that serves them

↓

Feudal society
In this phase, society is based upon a reciprocal economic and social system in which land is granted in return for some kind of service. For example, a king grants land to a nobleman in return for his military support; a nobleman grants land to peasants in return for taxes and tithes. Feudal society is characterized by a very strict class hierarchy

↓

Capitalism
In this phase, which follows industrialization, the principle economic goal is profit gained through capital. Society is divided between the owners of capital (the **bourgeoisie**) and those who do not own capital (the **proletariat**)

Economic forces

In each phase, **the economy** is the driving force in the development of human society. There are two principal aspects:

1 the forces of production, *and*   2 the relations of production.

Forces of production

These comprise: **labour power** (human capacity to work) and **means of labour** (technology, land, and so on).

By harnessing these together, humans are able to produce the basic necessities of survival – food, clothing, shelter, and so on.

Relations of production

Economic relations follow on from and reflect the forces of production. Relations of production include:

* the relations **between individuals and the forces of production** – does the individual own the factory or is he or she paid a wage to work in it?
* the relations **between individuals**, such as feudal lord and serf, factory owner and worker, and worker and worker.

The mode of production

Together the forces and relations of production create the characteristic **mode of production** of the society. For example, in the antebellum American South, the mode of production was characterized by:

* a dependence on land and labour, with minimal use of technology (= *the forces of production*)
* the institution of slavery, whereby the masters literally owned all the forces of production – both land and labour (= *relations of production*).

From time to time, the relations of production come to lag so far behind developments in the forces of production that they come into conflict with them. To resolve this conflict, the relations of production enter a period of a **rapid transformation** – a social and political revolution.

Commodities and value

Marx calls any goods or services produced under a particular mode of production that can be bought and sold **commodities**. Under the term 'commodity' he includes:

* physical merchandise, such as shoes, watches, works of art, and so on
* natural resources
* human labour power.

Commodities have two kinds of **value**:

* **Use value** They have value because they meet a certain need (e.g. a table meets the human need for something to have supper on)
* **Exchange value** They have value in that they can be exchanged for other commodities (e.g. a table might be 'worth' 50 loaves of bread or 10 bottles of wine, and so on).

As goods are not generally bartered directly one for another, the exchange value is expressed in money – the commodity's **price**.

The labour theory of value

What is it that gives a commodity its exchange value? Why is a table more valuable than, say, a loaf of bread?

For Marx, the crucial 'ingredient' is not so much the **raw materials** used to make the commodity, but the **amount of labour** that has been used to make it – a table takes much longer to make than a loaf of bread, and should therefore be more valuable and command a higher price.

In reality, this idea – that the origin of wealth lies in human labour – was not especially new, but Marx turned it to subversive, revolutionary ends.

● Human labour is what gives commodities their value

The mystery of surplus value

Surplus value is the core idea of Marx's analysis of capitalism, the 'invisible essence' that he sought to expose in the seemingly mysterious workings of capitalism.

* In earlier phases of economic development, the production and marketing of products is relatively straightforward and transparent. A producer sells a commodity for money and uses the money to buy another commodity. Marx expressed this in a simple notation:

$$C \rightarrow M \rightarrow C$$

* In capitalism, this is inverted. The capitalist invests money to produce commodities that he or she then sells to make a profit:

$$M \rightarrow C \rightarrow M_1$$

Marx called this 'extra' money, seemingly created out of thin air, surplus value.

Key term: capital
The term 'capital', in Marxist terms, refers to money used to create surplus value. Not all money is capital.

The mystery solved

Where does surplus value come from? How does the capitalist accumulate wealth? To answer this Marx turned to the labour theory of value. He argued that:

* The capitalist pays the workers a daily rate for their labour – the labour cost.
* However, in reality the workers work much longer and produce more commodities than they are paid for.
* The capitalist appropriates this extra free labour for himself in the form of gross profit.

7 Class

What is class?

Today sociologists use all sorts of indicators to determine class – family ('birth'), income, occupation, status, education, and so on. Although he never gave a formal definition of the word, Marx based his understanding of class solely on **economics**. We might sum this up as:

A class is made up of a group of individuals who share a common relation to economic production.

For example, in a feudal society the nobility (the elite minority) own the *means* of production – i.e. the land – while the peasantry (the majority) carry out the actual labour entailed in the production.

As this example suggests, the relations between the classes are always based on **injustice** and **exploitation** and their interests are necessarily **in conflict**. While the characteristics of the class system change through history, the injustice and exploitation remain. Outright, and even violent, conflict between the classes is inevitable and will eventually destroy the economic system from within.

In this chapter we will look at:

* the two main classes under capitalism – the bourgeoisie and the proletariat
* the role of ideology in the maintenance of the status quo
* class conflict and class consciousness
* the road to the classless society.

Class under capitalism

Under capitalism, the two opposing classes are:

1 the bourgeoisie

2 the proletariat.

The bourgeoisie

The bourgeoisie are the **owners of capital** – the minority, elite class that invests capital in the means of production (factories, machinery, etc.) and accumulates profit by **exploitation** of the proletariat. In the West, the bourgeoisie came to dominance in the late eighteenth century in the wake of the Industrial Revolution, as their *political* power came to reflect their *economic* power.

> The term 'bourgeoisie' derives from a French word describing the merchant class living in the towns and cities. Today, it is generally taken to be equivalent to 'middle class', although for Marx the meaning is much closer to 'upper, or dominant, class'.

The proletariat

The proletariat are the factory workers who do not own capital, and therefore must sell their labour power to the bourgeoisie.

In ancient Rome, the *proletarii* were the lowest class of citizens who owned little or no property.

Each class exists only in relation to the other – without one, the other could not exist. They are both mutually **dependent** and **antagonistic**.

Other 'classes'

Marx recognizes the existence of other classes under capitalism:

* The **lumpen proletariat**, for example, are an 'underclass' that do not engage in capitalist production at all – he called them the 'swindlers, confidence tricksters, brothel-keepers, rag-and-bone merchants, beggars and other flotsam of society'.
* The **petite bourgeoisie** are capitalists with smaller amounts of capital who are always at risk of being swallowed up by 'bigger fish'.

A Hegelian at heart, however, Marx views capitalism as defined by the relation between *two* great opposing forces.

Ideology

Why, historically, has the exploited class been so unwilling to challenge the 'upper class' and seize power?

According to Marx, the answer lies in the development of an oppressive **ideology** – a range of beliefs, ideas and laws in the **superstructure**, the overall message of which is that the class system is not a temporary, and hence transformable, phenomenon, but simply *how things are*.

Superstructure
The **superstructure**, remember, is the culture, laws, institutions, and so on that are built on the economic substructure of a society. The superstructure at once reflects, buttresses and disguises the crude economic relations.

● Why complain? This is just how things are

Victorian ideology

If we were to analyse the **conservative capitalist ideology** of Victorian Britain we might point to, for example:

* the institution of **Parliament**, which symbolized the enduring nature of the British polity
* the institution of the **monarchy**, which acted as a symbolic figurehead of a supposedly unified nation
* the **Church of England**, whose teachings typically emphasized continuity and the 'naturalness' of the social order.

**The rich man in his castle,
The poor man at his gate,
God made them high and lowly,
And ordered their estate.**

Victorian hymn, 'All Things Bright and Beautiful' (1848)

Class conflict

Marx saw the interests of the bourgeoisie and the proletariat as fundamentally opposed:

* The primary goal of the bourgeoisie is to **maximize profit** (and therefore to keep costs, including labour costs, down).
* The primary goal of the proletariat is to **maximize wages** and to improve working conditions.

80

This **fundamental tension** at the heart of capitalism would only intensify with time, Marx believed, and ensure that conflict, ultimately revolution, was inevitable.

The history of all hitherto-existing societies has been the history of class conflict.

The Communist Manifesto

Class consciousness

However, Marx argued that such conflict could bear fruit only once the working classes became self-aware – that is, of their shared interests as a class. He distinguished between:

* a class **'in itself'** – whereby individuals share economic interests but do not recognize their solidarity, *and*
* a class **'for itself'** – whereby the same individuals recognize their solidarity and are prepared to act collectively to achieve common goals.

Class consciousness, Marx thought, is primarily developed through **education**. This enables workers to strip away the illusions perpetuated by capitalist ideology and to perceive their actual predicament.

Marx himself expended a great deal of effort giving lectures to working men's groups.

Towards the classless society

Class agitation

Class conflict may take a number of forms, of varying degrees of intensity:

* the formation of **trade unions** and the use of tactics such as collective bargaining
* more dynamic expressions of solidarity such as **strikes** or sit-ins
* campaigns to improve workers' rights through legal reform
* political organization such as **workers' parties** (communist, socialist, etc.) and international movements such as the International Workingmen's Association
* **subversive** and/or **violent actions** against the state and its institutions, including revolution.

Of course, expressions of class conflict and consciousness can come from the other 'side' as well – for example, 'lock-outs', employers' organizations, and 'pro-capitalist' political parties.

The Communist Manifesto looks forward to the **classless society** as the final stage of historical economic development, after the proletarian revolution. Under communism, everyone …

✳ both has access to the means of production, *and*
✳ acts a producer.

The two opposing roles endemic to capitalism and earlier economic phases – worker and owner, ruled and ruler – collapse into one.

The Paris Commune

Marx did not see the establishment of a stable workers' state within his lifetime. However, he caught a glimpse of it in the Paris Commune of 1871. This was a **socialist government** that briefly ruled Paris during the upheavals of the Franco-Prussian War.

8 From alienation to freedom

The high cost of capitalism

In Marx's view, the individual is relatively **powerless** in the face of the economic structure he or she finds him- or herself in. See how Marx emphasizes this point: 'men *inevitably* enter definite relations, which are *independent of their will.*' We have no choice but to play by the rules we are given, if we want to survive. Under capitalism, however, this **loss of freedom** is intensified. The individual has even less control over his or her work and is oppressed by ever more stringent working conditions.

In Marx's vision of history, individuals are relatively powerless in the face of the economic structure they find themselves in ...

Marx believed, however, that **collectively** humans *can* take control of their lives and find freedom.

In this chapter we will look at:

* Marx's understanding of the term 'alienation' and how it comes about
* the related phenomenon of 'commodity fetishism'
* the illusory happiness provided by religion
* the core Marxist value of freedom.

Alienation

For Marx the feelings of alienation – *Entfremdung,* or estrangement –was an inevitable by-product of the capitalist system. Because **work is fundamental** to the human condition (we have to work in order to survive), we also derive much of our **happiness** and **satisfaction** from it and from working alongside others.

'Labour is the essence of man.'

Capitalism, however – and more particularly the factory system – alienates the worker from work in a number of ways:

* It alienates the worker from **working** – the factory system, by breaking up production into repetitive, meaningless tasks, denies the worker the satisfaction of engagement with a craft and a 'job well done'.

* It alienates the worker from the **product** – the worker has no real power over its design and making and probably does not even get to use or enjoy the product for him- or herself.
* It alienates the worker from **other workers** as well as employers – the emphasis on competition and menial tasks undermines the spirit of co-operation and comradeship.

The alienation of the bourgeoisie

Under capitalism, alienation is felt by everyone – both the proletariat and the bourgeoisie. However, according to Marx, the latter find both **pleasure** and **power** in these feelings – alienation enables them to feel both superior and divorced from the ugliness of capitalist production. By contrast, 'the class of the proletariat feels **annihilated**'.

Commodity fetishism

Alienation also underpins another key effect of living under capitalism – commodity fetishism. By this, Marx meant the way in which, under capitalism, commodities have a tendency to take on an **independent existence** and a **power** in their own right.

> To describe this effect, Marx borrowed the term 'fetishism' from studies of primitive religion where it is used to describe the worship of inanimate objects such as stones or trees.

Owing to this fetishization, the **realities** of capitalist production are **masked**. Celia Lury sums up Marx's idea neatly: 'Marx used the term fetishism of commodities to describe the disguising or masking of commodities whereby the appearance of goods hides the story of those who made them and how they made them.' (*Consumer Culture* 1996).

Brands and logos

From the twentieth century on, companies and advertisers have wilfully manipulated the phenomenon of commodity fetishization to sell more products. The mystique of the **brand** and the **logo** gives commodities a value that has very little to do with the thing itself – the material it is made from or the labour that has gone into it. In this way, consumers are prepared to spend money on an item about which in reality they know very little and are able to divorce themselves from the exploitation out of which it has possibly come. For example, a T-shirt made out of poor-quality material and produced in a sweatshop is magically transformed into a 'luxury' item by being printed with a logo.

The opium of the people

One of Marx's best-known statements is undoubtedly that '[religion] is the opium of the people' – by which he meant that, like the drug, religion dulls the pain of human existence and makes people forget their feelings of **alienation**.

The notion of religion as solace is as old as religion itself – the promise of reward in an afterlife makes present misery endurable. However, for Marx religion prevents people from becoming **fully conscious of their condition** and realizing that their 'sorrow' is not just a fact of life but remediable.

> **Religion is the sigh of the oppressed creature, the heart of a heartless world, and the soul of soulless conditions. It is the opium of the people.**

Introduction to *A Contribution to the Critique of Hegel's Philosophy of Right* (1844)

Religion as an instrument of oppression

For the atheist Marx, religion only appears to be a remedy for human alienation; in reality it is part of the cause. He believes that:

* Religion is part of the power structure that keeps people afraid, ignorant and oppressed and thus helps maintain the **status quo**.
* Religion is a **man-made 'fantasy'** that both reflects and compounds human beings' feelings of alienation.

In the communist state, religion will be abolished:

The abolition of religion as the illusory happiness of the people is the demand for their real happiness.

Introduction to *A Contribution to the Critique of Hegel's Philosophy of Right* (1844)

Freedom

In Marx's vision of the future communist society, freedom is a core value. This can be characterized in relation to many of the themes we have looked at in this chapter:

* The individual has **control over his or her own labour** and **finds fulfilment** in the work he or she produces.
* The individual will be freed from the dehumanizing **need to compete**.
* The individual will be freed from the **unfulfillable consumerist desire** created by commodity fetishism.
* The individual will be freed from the **illusion of religion** and instead will be fully in control of his or her own destiny.

Freedom in community

For Marx, true freedom, however, cannot exist in isolation, but only **in community**. The abolition of alienation will break down the artificial barriers between people and enable them to fulfil their human potential:

> **Only in community [has each] individual the means of cultivating his gifts in all directions; only in the community, therefore, is personal freedom possible.**

Karl Marx and Freidrich Engels, *The German Ideology* (1846)

In a capitalist society, the rights of the individual may be vaunted, but few people are truly free. In the communist society, the rights of the community will be more important, but everyone will enjoy true freedom.

9 From capitalism to communism

The hidden cracks in capitalism

For Marx, capitalism was an economic substructure that was riven with **internal flaws**, contradictions and paradoxes. While in the short term it might have *appeared* to flourish, benefiting the minority for whose advantage it had come into being, in the long term it was doomed. Eventually, as capitalism **spiralled into crisis**, the great mass of people would rise up to overthrow it.

Revolution, Marx believed, was thus inevitable, though he remained ambivalent about whether this would be by *violent* or peaceful means.

For Marx, capitalism was an economic structure that was riven with internal flaws

In this chapter we will look at Marx's ideas about:

* the inherent instability of capitalism
* the inevitability of revolution
* the 'dictatorship of the proletariat' as a stage on the road to pure communism
* the communist 'state'.

● For Marx, capitalism was an accident waiting to happen

The hidden cracks in capitalism

Marx believed that capitalism was inherently unstable and would be torn apart by its contradictions:

* To **maximize profits** employers needed to pay their factory workers as little as possible; yet at the same time they needed the mass of workers to be **better paid** so that they could buy their commodities.

* Fierce **competition** between factory owners meant that profits would always fall over time; **overproduction** – the flooding of the market with identical or similar goods – would have the same result.

* For much the same reasons, workers' wages would always be under a downward pressure, leading to the **ever greater impoverishment** of the proletariat and **greater divisions** between the 'haves' and 'have-nots'.

* Capitalism is based on destructive **violence** – the violence of exploitation and the violence of the class struggle.

Wasted labour

Another major problem with capitalism, Marx thought, is that many commodities do not have any real 'use value'. Manufacturers churn out goods not so much because there is necessarily a **use** for them but primarily **to sell them for a profit**. Moreover, because there is no overall organization of the economy, manufacturers tend to produce a superabundance of identical or similar products. For Marx, this meant that what should be socially valuable labour was being wasted.

As capitalism develops, Marx thought, these internal contradictions would deepen and the economy would lurch from booms to busts of increasing frequency and intensity. Capitalism would eventually consume itself and revolution would be ignited.

Revolution

For Marx, revolution was inevitable and must arise from the working classes themselves. In his preface to the *Rule and Regulations of the International Workingmen's Association* (1867) he proclaimed:

'[...] the emancipation of the working classes must be conquered by the working classes themselves; [...] the struggle for the emancipation of the working classes means not a struggle for class privileges and monopolies, but for equal rights and duties, and the abolition of all class rule [...]'

History had shown, Marx thought, that **middle-class liberals** were not to be trusted as allies as sooner or later they would turn against the interests of working people and create the revolution in their own image. Marx was similarly mistrustful of the **peasantry**, who, he thought, also tended towards conservative values.

Revolutionary violence

Marx believed that **force** would be necessary if capitalism was to be overthrown. As we have seen, *The Communist Manifesto*, for example, finishes on a menacing note:

'[The communists] openly declare that their ends can be attained only by the forcible overthrow of all existing social conditions. Let the ruling classes tremble at a Communist revolution [...]'

To what **degree** of force Marx is here referring is a matter of debate. Because he saw human history itself as a kind of battle of wills, the communist revolution itself would be a kind of final imposition of will by the working classes. However, the question as to whether Marx would have accepted **large-scale violence** – i.e. widespread bloodshed – is an open one.

After the revolution

While Marx was thorough in his investigations into capitalism, beyond broad ideals and aims he was understandably much more vague about how **communism** would function. However, he realized that a **pure communist society** would not be immediately achievable but would be an ideal that the post-revolutionary **socialist society** would have to work towards.

The dictatorship of the proletariat

Marx thought that during this intermediary phase the working class would remain in power, and he called this the 'dictatorship of the proletariat'.

> By dictatorship, Marx did not mean that a small elite would be in power, but that the working class as a group would be in control within the context of a democratic state. He saw capitalism as a 'dictatorship of the bourgeoisie'.

Under the dictatorship of the proletariat:

* The state would control the 'proceeds of labour' – i.e. food, clothes and other commodities.
* Out of these the state would support public services, look after those unable to work and invest in further production.
* Anything that remained would be shared among the workers according to how hard they had worked.

Marx wrote about these ideas in an open letter known as the 'Critique of the Gotha Programme' in 1875.

Marx believed that the transformation of capitalism under the 'workers' state' would be difficult because the new society would be 'economically, morally and intellectually […] still stamped with the birth marks of the old society from whose womb it emerges'.

The 'communist state'

While the state clearly has an important role to play under the dictatorship of the proletariat, eventually, Marx believed, its powers would dwindle.

Marx argued that historically the function of the state was 'to keep the great majority of producers beneath the yoke of a small minority' and that, as such, it always had a tendency towards oppression. In a communist society, it would become purely administrative.

For this reason, Marx's ideas share something in common with **anarchism**. Both shared a vision of a community in which the state played no or only a minimal role.

Strictly speaking, the term communist state is an oxymoron; post-revolutionary states in the twentieth century called themselves 'socialist states' (or republics).

Marx's ideas about what the future communist society would look like can seem vague. It was this ideological near-vacuum that was filled by the ideas of the communist thinkers and revolutionaries that followed in his wake. The communist regimes of the twentieth century were less realizations of a Marx-derived blueprint than extemporized political experiments.

● Marx believed that under communism the state would wither away and people would rule themselves

10 Impact

Marxism today

No single thinker perhaps had a greater impact on the course of twentieth-century history than Karl Marx. Within decades of his death, a revolutionary Marxist party in Russia – the Bolsheviks – had orchestrated a **violent revolution** that established the world's first 'communist state' – the **Union of Soviet Socialist Republics** – though whether Marx would have recognized the USSR as such is debatable.

Subsequent decades, moreover, saw the development of a near-cataclysmic, worldwide **ideological clash** between the forces of capitalism and communism of a kind predicted in the pages of *Capital*.

No single thinker perhaps had a greater impact on the course of twentieth-century history than Karl Marx

However, in 1991 the collapse of the USSR seemed suddenly to consign both communism and Marx to the past. His ideas, born out of the industrial age, were redundant in the post-modern, post-industrial one, or so it seemed.

In this chapter we will look at:

* the rise of 'communist states' in the twentieth century
* the development of 'neo-Marxist' ideas
* critiques of Marxism
* the continuing relevance of Marxism.

Communism in the twentieth century

The 'spectre of communism' looms large in the history of the twentieth century:

1917   The Russian Revolution, led by Vladimir Lenin, brings about **the world's first 'communist'** (or socialist) **state**; in other countries the fear of the exportation of the 'red menace' becomes pervasive over the following decades.

1936–39   The Spanish Civil War becomes the focal point of the **ideological conflict** between fascism and communism.

After 1945 The Soviet victory over Nazi Germany in the Second World War enabled it to help establish 'communist states' in many eastern European countries (the **Eastern bloc**).

1946	The beginning of the **Cold War** – the ideological conflict between the 'communist states' led by the Soviet Union and Western capitalist states led by the USA sees heightened **military tension** (together with the threat of nuclear conflict), **economic and cultural rivalry** (e.g. the 'space race') and **proxy wars** (e.g. the Korean War, 1950–53; the Vietnam War, 1955–75).
1949	The victory of the communists in the Chinese Civil War establishes the communist **People's Republic of China**.
1989	Revolutions overthrow communist regimes across Eastern Europe, and the dissolution of the Soviet Union in 1991 causes a **worldwide retreat of communism** and the end of the Cold War.

Critiques of Marxism

Marx's ideas have attracted a great deal of criticism across the political spectrum and on economic, sociological, political and ethical grounds.

Economic

* The **labour theory of value** – that the value of commodities lies solely in the amount of labour put in by the workers – has been widely contested. Many economists have pointed to other sources of value:
  » the labour of the capitalists and managers
  » the judgement of the consumer of a commodity's usefulness or desirability.

Sociological

* **Dialectical materialism** overemphasizes the role played by economics in driving societal change; other aspects such as culture and ideas are also key.

Political and ethical

* Anarchists such as Bakunin argued that the **'dictatorship of the proletariat'** would inevitably become dominated by a tyrannous 'new aristocracy'.
* The totalitarian regimes established by 'communist' dictators such as Stalin and Mao proved the dangers inherent in Marxist ideas.

Animal Farm

George Orwell's satirical novella *Animal Farm* (1945) famously depicts the dangers implicit in communist revolution owing to a **corrupt leadership**. Inspired by the ideas of a kindly old pig named Old Major – who seems to represent both Marx and Lenin – the animals rebel against the farmer and take over their farm. Under the leadership of younger pigs, however, the revolution's original ideals ('All animals are equal') are debased ('but some are more equal than others'). Orwell was a democratic socialist and used his 'fairy story' to attack the Stalinist corruption of Marx's ideas.

Marxism: an evolving concept

Through the twentieth century and beyond 'neo-Marxist' political thinkers, reformers and revolutionaries have interpreted, adapted, developed and (arguably) corrupted Marx's ideas.

Marxist-Leninism

Marxist-Leninists (following the ideas of the Russian revolutionary Vladimir Lenin) argue that violent revolution, led by an elite vanguard, is the necessary precursor to the socialist state and to communism beyond.

Democratic socialism

Democratic socialists believe that it is possible to move towards Marx's ideal state by means of a **process of reform** within the capitalist system. The movement developed in the late nineteenth century and continues to flourish within many Western socialist parties today, such as the British Labour Party.

Trotskyism

The Russian revolutionary Leon Trotsky emphasized **mass democracy** within the socialist state and the promotion of revolution **internationally** ('permanent revolution').

Maoism

The Chinese revolutionary leader Mao Zedong developed Marxist thought to make it more appropriate for a largely **peasant-based economy** and emphasized the key role of **military tactics** in bringing about revolution.

Eco-Marxism/Socialism

Marxist ideas have also been taken up by some environmentalists who argue that the best way to save the planet is to end capitalism, which exploits the environment as well as workers.

The continuing relevance of Marx

In 1989–91 the collapse of the socialist republics across Europe was heralded by some as the triumph of liberal democracy and the **defeat of communism**. One US thinker, Francis Fukuyama, even spoke of 'the end of history' – by which he meant the end of the ideological struggle between capitalism and communism. Marx and his ideas, it seemed, had become **redundant**.

However, since then the seemingly unstoppable rise of globalized capitalism has once again **brought Marx and his ideas to the fore**. Debate has focused on issues such as:

* the **exploitation of workers** in the new capitalist economies such as India and Brazil, and notably the use of child labour

* the **global consumer culture** with its 'fetishized' emphasis on branding and logos

* the **2007 economic crisis** – which reinvigorated ideas about the inherent **instability of capitalism** (see Chapter 9).

Urgent questions about the 'necessary' reform of the economic system and even about 'revolution' have again come to the fore.

The future revolution

Neo-Marxists debate about where any future revolution is likely to take place. Is there potential either for reform or revolution in the post-industrial countries of the West such as the USA, Japan or the UK, where capitalism is so deep-rooted? Or is the best chance for a radical challenge to capitalism to be found in so-called **'peripheral' countries** such as India or Brazil, where capitalism is still emerging?

Of course, many continue to contest Marx's ideas about capitalism and argue that it still offers the best hope for a flourishing global economy. Marx and his ideas live on, continuing to provoke and inspire in equal measure.

Further reading

For those wanting to explore Marx's ideas further, *The Communist Manifesto* (Penguin, 2004) is, of course, a good place to start – in it, you will discover the **fiery utopian vision** that inspired not only Marx but the political thinkers and revolutionaries who followed in his wake. For those who want to dig deeper into his **economic theories**, the first volume of *Capital* (Penguin, 2004) provides the best way into his extraordinary achievement. Those who want to know more about his **life** can do no better than to read Francis Wheen's accessible biography (Fourth Estate, new edition 2010).

Internet resources include: www.marxists.org (includes online texts by Marx).

You might like to visit the Karl Marx Museum in Trier, Germany, which has an excellent exhibition on his life and works, or pay homage at his tomb in Highgate Cemetery, London.